D0859874

EXOTIC FRUITS
& VEGETABLES

PHOTOGRAPHY AND DESIGN
BY KOREN TRYGG
TEXT BY LUCY POSHEK

ANTIOCH GOURMET
GIFT BOOKS

Published by Antioch Publishing Company
Yellow Springs, Ohio 45387

ISBN 0-89954-237-9

EXOTIC FRUITS & VEGETABLES

Printed and bound in the U.S.A.

CONTENTS

INTRODUCTION

Exotic fruits and vegetables are more widely available now than ever before—so plentiful, in fact, that some foods previously considered exotic have by now become familiar sights in most supermarkets.

Why this sudden bounty of exciting new produce? For one thing, many exotic fruits and vegetables can now be grown locally, enabling us to savor them at their best. At the same time, consumers are growing more aware of the healthful effects of fresh, natural fruits and vegetables. The demand for exotic produce has been particularly high because of increasing international and ethnic influences in our cuisine.

Deciding exactly which fruits and vegetables are "exotic" depends largely upon the region where one lives. The mango, for instance, has long been considered a staple in the tropical world, but most Westerners are barely acquainted with this delicious fruit. Lychees have been highly regarded by the Chinese for over two thousand years, while celeriac and kohlrabi have been used in European kitchens since early times.

Many tropically-grown fruits and vegetables were first spread throughout the world by the early explorers. Others, such as Belgian endive, were discovered quite by accident as recently as the nineteenth century. And the

kiwi only made its way out of New Zealand in the past two decades when its original name—the Chinese gooseberry—was changed during one of the most successful marketing campaigns in the history of food.

We often shy away from exotic fruits and vegetables, unsure of their flavors, preparation or uses. Some, like the mango and papaya, are best eaten unadulterated with little more than a squeeze of lime. Others, such as the kiwano, should be flavored first, or served with other foods. Still others, like the star-shaped carambola, are most striking as a garnish. And then there are those few homely yet flavorful fruits and vegetables which are better tasted and not seen. The passion fruit, for example, is not very glamorous looking, but only a small amount of the juice creates a wonderful flavoring for drinks, ices, and creams.

The following fruits and vegetables, all with their own refreshing personalities, can be found in most markets today. Experience their luscious textures, subtle flavors, and fragrant aromas, and discover a whole new world of culinary sensations.

*"Nature alone is antique
and the oldest art a mushroom."*

THOMAS CARLYLE

EXOTIC FRUITS

ASIAN PEAR

Brought to America by Chinese prospectors during the Gold Rush, Asian pears are now grown in California and the Pacific Northwest. There are at least twenty-five varieties, but most Asian pears share in common the juiciness of a pear with the shape and crispness of an apple. They are hard when ripe and have a refreshing, subtle sweetness. Like apples, Asian pears are one of the few fruits that store well. Available midsummer through early spring, they are usually sold ripe and ready to eat.

Asian pears are good simply unpeeled, eaten out of hand, or sliced and added to salads, or served with soft dessert cheese. In Asia, the fruit is traditionally eaten at the end of the meal—peeled and cut into thin horizontal slices. You can also poach them like pears, but allow for longer cooking time.

CARAMBOLA

This striking tropical fruit is also known as the starfruit, because it has five prominent ridges which reveal a star-shaped pattern when cut crosswise. Golden yellow when ripe, its flesh is juicy and ranging in taste from sweet to tart. Sweet carambolas—those with thicker, wider ribs—have overtones of orange-pineapple, while the tart varieties with very narrow ribs have more of a fruity-lemon flavor.

Imported from Java and the tropics between late summer and winter, carambolas can be bought when green and stored at room temperature until they turn yellow. Once ripe, they can be refrigerated for a week or so. When ready to serve, simply crosscut them without peeling the thin, waxy skin. Remove the seeds and trim off the thin, brown edge of each rib, if desired.

The golden star-shaped slices make an impressive garnish to entrées, salads, desserts and beverages. Carambolas are also good cooked—sautéed with shellfish or thrown into stir-fries. They are a good source of vitamin C.

CHERIMOYA

Cherimoyas, or custard apples, resemble light green pine cones or artichokes without the protruding leaves. They vary in size and can range from round to heart-shaped. Their creamy flesh, somewhat juicy and custard-like in texture, covers large black seeds. The flavor is a delicate, tropical blend of banana, pineapple, and vanilla custard.

Native to the Andes, cherimoyas are now grown in subtropical regions around the world. Look for them from November through May. Their size doesn't indicate their quality, but they should have a uniformly green color. Firm cherimoyas should be kept at room temperature until ripe, when the skin yields to gentle pressure. You can either cut the fruit into halves or quarters and scoop out the pulp, or peel the skin away in strips first. Remove the seeds and brush with lemon juice to prevent darkening.

Use fresh cherimoya slices in fruit salads, or purée them for sorbets, ice creams and sherbets, no-bake pies or blended drinks. This luscious fruit is best eaten uncooked.

Mark Twain often described the cherimoya as "deliciousness itself."

FEIJOA

This small, oval-shaped relative of the guava is also known as the pineapple guava. Native to South America, feijoas are now grown around the world. In fact, the evergreens from which the gray-green fruits grow are considered ornamental trees in some parts of the world.

Feijoas should be eaten only when they are slightly soft and have a strong lime-pineapple aroma. Their flesh is pale yellow with a granular texture and a sweet-tart taste. Each jelly-like center is dotted with tiny seeds. When ready to serve, simply cut the fruit in half and scoop the pulp out with a spoon. You can also peel the skin off and cut the fruit into slices. Brush cut feijoas with lemon juice to prevent darkening.

Fresh feijoas are good in fruit salads or puréed for ices. Like the guava, their high pectin content makes them a natural in jams and jellies. They are available from early spring to early summer and then again in the fall.

GUAVA

Native to tropical America, guavas were spread throughout the world by the early explorers. There are about one hundred fifty guava species, widely ranging in appearance and taste. Guavas can be round or pear-shaped; the flavor can vary from strawberry to pineapple to banana, from sharply tart to sweet. Their flesh can be white, pink or yellow. All varieties are very fragrant.

Guavas are available from August through October. Select fruits which are as yellow as possible or they might

be too tart. Let them ripen at room temperature until they are somewhat soft to the touch. The whole fruit is edible, but they are usually peeled first. After cutting, sprinkle with lemon juice to prevent discoloration.

Guavas can be eaten out of hand, added to fruit salads, or puréed. They can also be stewed and made into chutney or jelly. In some tropical countries guava jelly is traditionally eaten with cream cheese. Canned guavas are quite good and are also rich in minerals and vitamin C.

KIWANO

The kiwano, or horned melon, originated in Africa but is now grown in California and New Zealand. Altogether, this fruit is not for the faint of heart. Its yellow skin is covered with spiky protuberances, and inside is a jelly-like, lime green pulp. When ripe, the fruit tastes like a cross between cucumber and lime.

Rather than being eaten alone, the tart green fruit of the kiwano is best when puréed and sweetened for fruit sauces, dressings, sorbets, and drinks. The scooped-out shell makes a conversational vessel for fruit salads. Available year-round, kiwanos keep well and should not be refrigerated.

"There is greater relish for the earliest fruit of the season."

MARTIAL

13

Mango

Kumquat

Tamarillo

Pepin

Asian pear

Lychee

Kiwi

Papaya

Plantain

Passion fruit

Feijoa

Kiwano

KIWI

The kiwifruit was first cultivated in New Zealand, where it was known as the Chinese gooseberry. In the 1970's the fruit was renamed after New Zealand's native bird (which it does slightly resemble if you added legs to it!). Suddenly, kiwis were in great demand and much used in nouvelle cuisine. Now the fruit is widely grown year-round.

The green flesh of the kiwi is marked with a delicate swirl of tiny, black edible seeds, best shown off when cut crosswise. Fresh kiwi slices make a pretty garnish for salads, entrées, tarts and cheesecakes. In New Zealand they are served with a creamy meringue dessert called Pavlova. Kiwis have a wonderful, sweet-tart flavor and are one of the most nutritious fruits around. They are very high in vitamin C.

These fuzzy little fruits are incredibly easy to prepare: Simply peel the brown skin off and cut the fruit into thin slices; or just cut the kiwi in half and scoop the flesh out with a spoon. Kiwis are best eaten fresh because their bright green color fades when cooked. They can be kept for weeks in the refrigerator and are ripe when slightly soft to the touch.

"We cannot eat the fruit while the tree is in blossom."

BENJAMIN DISRAELI

KUMQUAT

The kumquat, which means "golden orange," was first cultivated in China but was not introduced to the Western world until the nineteenth century. These tiny, thin-skinned fruits look like miniature oranges. It was once the fashionable custom to place whole kumquat plants on the table during dinner so that guests could pick the fruits fresh off the tree.

Kumquats grow year-round and make an excellent garnish for entrées, appetizers and salads. They are usually eaten whole, peel and all, and are unique in that their skin is sweet whereas their fruit is tart. You may prefer to blanch them first to soften the skin. They are less sour if preserved in honey or sugar (a Chinese tradition), cooked in syrup, or made into marmalade. Kumquats keep several weeks when refrigerated.

LYCHEE

The lychee (sometimes spelled "litchi") is a small tropical fruit with a hard, knobby shell that ranges from pink-yellow to reddish-brown as it ripens. The shell pulls away easily to reveal translucent, grape-flavored flesh surrounding a single pit. Only the sweet pulp is eaten.

Native to China, lychees have been regarded as one of the finest delicacies for two thousand years. They were so popular in ancient times that couriers rushed fresh lychees straight to the Imperial court. Today they are grown in tropical regions around the world.

Available in midsummer, from June to July, lychees

are sold both fresh and canned. Fresh lychees last several weeks when refrigerated or several months when frozen. High in vitamin C, they are good eaten out of hand, in fruit salads, chicken salads, and ices.

MANGO

Also called "the king of the fruits" and "the apple of the tropics," mangoes are often disliked by Westerners only because Westerners wind up with a bad, fibrous, or unripe variety. But mangoes are as much a mainstay of the tropics as the apple is elsewhere. In Hawaii, the old-timers even refer to time as "mango seasons." A good, ripe mango will practically melt in your mouth with its luscious flavor.

There are many varieties grown in Asia and India, and Indian mangoes are considered the finest. Available from midwinter through fall, the fruits vary greatly in size, shape, and color, including green, yellow, orange and crimson. Their skin color does not at all indicate ripeness. A ripe mango is somewhat soft all over and has a fragrant aroma near the stem end. The yellow-orange-colored flesh is somewhat stringy, deliciously juicy and messy when ripe, with the taste of spicy melons. But when not fully ripe, the flavor is bitter and turpentine-like.

Ripe mangoes are best eaten chilled, the skin peeled off (though it is edible), and the large pit removed. They are a natural with chicken, wonderful in fresh fruit salads, and delicious when stewed into jams and chutneys.

PAPAYA

When Christopher Columbus discovered papayas in the Caribbean he called them the "fruit of angels," and for good reason. There is nothing more delicious for breakfast than a perfectly ripe, chilled papaya sliced in half and sprinkled with fresh lime juice.

Grown year-round in the tropics, papayas have a soft, smooth texture and very delicate flavor. They range in size from a pear-shaped melon to a ten-pound variety, and their pulp can be yellow, orange or salmon-colored.

Allow papayas to ripen at room temperature until the skin has turned from green to at least half yellow and becomes slightly soft all over. Refrigerate before serving, then slice the fruit in half, scooping out the black, edible pepper-flavored seeds. The skin is not eaten. The halves can be eaten alone or stuffed with salads. Papaya can also be baked, grilled, sautéed or puréed. Try wrapping fresh papaya slices in prosciutto for a tasty appetizer.

One of the most healthful of all fruits, papayas are a good source of vitamins A and C. They are also an excellent aid to digestion as they contain a digestive enzyme called papain.

"The weakest kind of fruit
Drops earliest to the ground."

WILLIAM SHAKESPEARE

PASSION FRUIT

Native to Brazil, this fragrant tropical fruit was given its name because Spanish missionaries to South America believed that the different parts of its flowers symbolized the Passion of Christ.

The passion fruit can be purplish-brown, red or gold in color and has a leathery, dimpled shell. In fact, the more wrinkled the skin is, the better the fruit. Inside is an unattractive, greenish pulp surrounding many edible seeds. But its flowery-lime flavor is remarkably fragrant when added with a sweetener to drinks, jellies, ices, whipped cream, and sauces. The flavor of passion fruit is so intense that it is best puréed into a flavoring agent and used in small amounts.

Available mostly in summer, passion fruits are grown throughout the tropical world. Once ripe, the fruit can be refrigerated for about one week. You can also store whole passion fruits, or the scooped-out pulp, for several months in a freezer container. When ready to serve, cut the fruit in half and scoop out the pulp and seeds. They are best consumed fresh rather than cooked. Five to six fruits will yield only about one-half cup of pulp.

"Passion is the fruit of life."
SOO LING

PEPINO

The pepino resembles a tear-drop-shaped cucumber (its name means "cucumber" in Spanish), but the skin is yellow with purple streaks. The texture of the fruit is melon-like, and the flavor is very mild. Cultivated year-round in the subtropics, pepinos are a popular fruit in the Orient and particularly Japan.

Keep unripe pepinos—still firm and streaked with green—at room temperature until the green turns to yellow and the fruit yields to gentle pressure. They are best chilled, cut in half, seeds removed, with the pulp scooped out of the thin skin. A squeeze of fresh lemon or lime juice enhances the flavor. The halved fruit can also be stuffed with other ingredients or served with frozen yogurt. Pepinos are best when uncooked.

PLANTAIN

Out of four hundred varieties of bananas that are grown year-round in the tropical Americas, the plantain is one of the most common. Also known as the "cooking banana" and "the potato of the tropics," the plantain looks like a large banana with tapering ends.

Plantains can be eaten at each stage of maturity, but they must be cooked first. When green, unripe and starchy, they are good sliced and fried like potato chips. When brown-ripe and sweet, they can be sautéed in butter, baked, broiled or grilled, and served with meat, poultry or seafood. Black-ripe plantains, the sweetest, are best sautéed in butter as a dessert and flavored with cinnamon

23

sugar or brown sugar.

Unlike American-style bananas, plantains are hard to peel. Try slicing off the tips and cutting them crosswise into half. Then make four lengthwise slits and pull the skin away.

TAMARILLO

Also called the tree tomato, the tamarillo is a tropical relative of the tomato and kiwi. A glossy, egg-shaped fruit, it can be either yellow (the sweet variety) or red with orange flesh and edible purple seeds.

You can use tamarillos as you would use tomatoes in salads and sandwiches, but the fruit is usually best eaten cooked, as its flesh is slightly tart. They can be stewed into chutneys, puréed into sauces, sautéed, or baked in syrup. Tamarillos are especially good cooked with cinnamon and sugar. If eaten raw, they must be ripe and soft to the touch and should be sweetened to bring out their best flavor. Always remove the shiny skin before eating, and be careful to avoid stains on the hands from the red fruit.

Native to South America, the tamarillo is now grown mostly in California and New Zealand from early spring through fall.

*"But the fruit that can fall without shaking
Indeed is too mellow for me."*

LADY MARY WORTLEY MONTAGU, 1837

EXOTIC VEGETABLES

BELGIAN ENDIVE

This tightly-wrapped bundle of satiny leaves, also known as witloof, is a sophisticated member of the chicory family. (Curly endive, or chicory, is a different member of the same family.) The sleek leaves, or stalks, are pleasant and slightly bitter tasting. They derive their light creamy color from growing in the dark. It is said that a nineteenth-century Belgian gardener first found the white leaves sprouting from a chicory root in his cellar. Belgium still leads in the production of endive, but the United

States and rest of Europe are also growing it now. It is available year-round but is best from autumn to spring. The leaves of Belgian endive are good added raw to salads or arranged pinwheel-like on a plate as an appetizer with a light, delicate dip such as crab dip. Belgian endive can also be braised but should not be cooked in an iron skillet or the leaves will discolor.

To prepare Belgian endive, trim the base and remove the core. Cut it crosswise into rounds or separate the leaves and use them whole.

BOK CHOY

A member of the *Brassica* family, bok choy (also called mustard greens) has juicy white stems and mild-flavored, dark green leaves. In looks and taste, bok choy most closely resembles Swiss chard.

Available year-round, bok choy is especially popular in Oriental cooking. Since they cook quickly when cut into small slices, the leaves and stalks are excellent for stir-fries. Thin ribbons of bok choy leaves can also be added to Oriental soups. Or, simply boil the leaves until just tender and serve them alone with butter, salt and pepper. Raw, flowering bok choy makes a good garnish in salads.

"That's mighty tasty."

STEVE LARWOOD

CELERIAC

This variety of celery is cultivated not for its stalks but rather for its tuberous root-base. Also known as celery root, celeriac is not very elegant looking. Covering the lumpy globe root is a coarse brown skin with tiny rootlets hanging from the bottom. But once cut into slices and peeled, the earthy, celery-and-pepper-flavored root is good both raw and cooked. It has long been used in European cooking.

Although celeriac is considered a winter vegetable, it is available most of the year. Look for small roots up to one pound. After cutting, immediately brush the root with water and lemon juice to prevent browning. If serving raw, cut the root into julienne strips (blanching helps to soften them somewhat), or grate the root and add to other vegetables with a vinaigrette. Like celery, celeriac makes a wonderful addition to soups or stews. For another variation, try cooking equal amounts of celeriac with potatoes and then purée them together.

FENNEL

Fennel, also known as Florence fennel or *finocchio*, has been a favorite vegetable in Italian dishes—from appetizers to desserts—since ancient times. It is widely grown from fall through spring in Europe and the United States. Its celery-like stalks, bulbous base, and feathery green fronds have a faint sweet-licorice flavor. When served raw, the flavor of fennel is strongest and helps to cleanse the palate. Cooking mellows it into a more delicate, sweet flavor.

Fennel should be refrigerated and used within a few days. To prepare the bulb, remove the core and first layer of the base. Then cut the bulb into wedges. The wedges can be sautéed, cooked with roasts, grilled, or julienned and blanched for a vinaigrette salad. Fennel can serve as an exciting substitute for celery in most recipes. All parts of the vegetable are marvelous for flavoring soups, stews and marinara sauces. A few crushed fennel seeds will enhance the flavor even further. When the bulb is sold with its stalks, the leaves make a delicate, dill-like garnish.

JERUSALEM ARTICHOKE

Jerusalem artichokes are a misnomer, as these tubers are neither from Jerusalem nor related to the globe artichoke. They are native to the American Indians and were brought to Europe by the early explorers. These vegetables may resemble the globe artichoke in flavor, but they are actually members of the sunflower family. Lately they have been more accurately marketed as sunchokes, or sunroots.

Look for Jerusalem artichokes from autumn to spring, when they are sweetest. They can range in color from beige to brownish-red, but avoid artichokes with wrinkled or knobby skins. You can leave the skin on or off, but be sure to scrub the unpeeled ones thoroughly. Brush peeled artichokes with lemon-water to prevent browning. You can also cook them until just tender and remove the peels after cooking.

These tasty tubers can be baked, boiled, steamed or

fried. Like potatoes, they can also be roasted with meat. They are good mashed to a purée for soup (a favorite of Charles Dickens), served cold with a vinaigrette, or hot with butter and fresh herbs. Shredded and mixed with a mayonnaise dressing, Jerusalem artichokes make a refreshing salad.

JICAMA

Jicama is a Mexican root that grows up to six pounds and looks like a giant brown turnip. Its thick skin and ugly exterior hide a refreshingly crisp, mildly sweet white flesh that resembles water chestnuts. Jicama does in fact make an inexpensive substitute for water chestnuts in most recipes. It is very popular in Asia and the Pacific; and perhaps even more so in Mexico, where jicama is a common staple. It is a Mexican custom to serve sticks of jicama sprinkled with chili powder, lime juice, and salt.

Uncut jicama stores well in a cool, dry place for several weeks. Peel the tough skin with a strong knife and cut into whatever shapes you desire. Brush with lemon-water to prevent browning.

Raw jicama makes a very refreshing addition to any salad. It is also a wonderful accompaniment with almost any dip. The root can be cooked (surprisingly, it retains its crispy texture), but is usually better combined with other vegetables. A one-pound jicama yields about three cups when peeled and chopped.

Bok choy

Radicchio

Jerusalem
artichoke

Kohlrabi

Celeriac

Jicama

Belgian
endive

Fennel

Exotic
mushrooms

KOHLRABI

Kohlrabi means "cabbage-turnip" in German and has been used in European kitchens since the time of Charlemagne. Its homely, globe-shaped bulb does indeed taste like cabbage and look like a turnip. But kohlrabi, a member of the *Brassica* family, is actually a thick stem that forms above the ground. The bulb can range from light green to magenta, with a slightly sweet, crisp bite. The leaves can be cooked like kale, but their taste is a bit sharper.

This delicious vegetable is available throughout most of the year, but is best from June through October. Pick small to medium-sized bulbs for the sweetest flavor. Except for small kohlrabies, the peel of the bulb is usually removed before serving. Raw kohlrabi has a stronger flavor than when cooked and is good served in salads, with dips, or grated into coleslaw with carrots. If boiled, kohlrabi should be cooked for 25 to 30 minutes and served with butter or a cream sauce.

EXOTIC MUSHROOMS

Although mushrooms are technically a fungi, they are often considered a vegetable. And adventurous cooks are finding many vegetable-like uses for exotic, or specialty mushrooms, many of which grow wild.

Like common button mushrooms, exotic mushrooms should be firm and plump when bought fresh, then washed carefully and used quickly. Dried mushrooms should be softened up by soaking in hot water for thirty

minutes first. All mushrooms are most sublime when prepared simply—sautéed in butter for a few minutes and
eaten alone, or added to entrées, stews, soups, omelettes,
stir-fries, pizzas, and pastas.

The following are only a few of the most popular and
scrumptious varieties among over two thousand species of
exotic mushrooms.

Chantrelle - These frilly, trumpet-shaped wild mushrooms can be found in many colors and possess the subtle
aroma of apricots. Available from summer through midwinter, chantrelles are very popular in Europe.

Enoki - With their long stems and tiny caps, enoki
mushrooms look like large bean sprouts. Unlike most
exotic mushrooms, enokis are best eaten raw or heated
only briefly.

Morel - A much sought-after wild spring delicacy,
morels resemble a honeycombed sponge. They vary in
color from cream to black, with a meaty texture and rich,
earthy flavor. Always wash morels carefully, trim off their
tough stems, and cook them first.

Oyster - Oyster mushrooms range greatly in size and
color, but usually grow in clusters and have silky caps.
Their subtle seafood flavor is more delicate when cooked
or sautéed; raw, the taste is sharper.

Porcini - Also called *cèpes*, porcini have spongy layers
of holes instead of gills under the plump, brown caps.
Harvested wild in the fall, they have a pronounced flavor
and meaty texture.

Shiitake - A Chinese-Japanese fungi, shiitake are

shaped like large parasols and have a rich, hearty flavor.
Used in Oriental cooking for over two thousand years.
Their stems are tough but add an exotic flavoring to
soups.

Wood Ear - These flowery-shaped mushrooms are
widely used in Chinese cooking. They possess a rich,
incredibly buttery flavor.

RADICCHIO

A member of the chicory family, radicchio (pronounced "rahd-EEK-ee-o") is the Italian word for
chicory. Available year-round, radicchio has always been
a favorite leafy vegetable in Europe. Its burgundy leaves
and contrasting white ribs create a colorful garnish and
striking addition to tossed salads. The leaves have a slight
bittersweet flavor which is complemented by vinaigrette.
Radicchio is also excellent when cut into wedges, brushed
with olive oil, grilled, and served warm.

To prepare radicchio, remove the white central core,
separate the leaves, rinse and blot dry. If grilling, remove
the core and cut the head into thick wedges.

*"No vegetable exists which is not better
slightly undercooked."*

JAMES BEARD

Plantain Chips

green plantains
vegetable oil
salt

*Peel plantains and slice very thinly. Heat oil
¼-inch deep in a skillet over medium-high heat. Place
plantain slices in hot oil and cook 2 to 4 minutes on
each side until golden. Drain on paper towels;
sprinkle with salt.*

Celeriac-Kohlrabi Salad

1 medium celeriac, peeled and grated
1 medium kohlrabi, peeled and grated
1 medium carrot, grated
¼ cup (2 fl. oz.) mayonnaise
1 tsp. (¾ Br. tsp.) Dijon mustard
1 tsp. (¾ Br. tsp.) dried tarragon
2 tsp. (1½ Br. tsp.) pine nuts, crushed (opt.)
freshly ground pepper to taste

*Combine grated vegetables in a bowl. In a separate
bowl, mix remaining ingredients until well blended.
Add to vegetables and toss. Serves 2.*

Belgian Endive & Prosciutto Appetizer

1 head Belgian endive, core removed
3 oz. prosciutto
½ cup (4 fl. oz.) shredded radicchio
½ cup (4 fl. oz.) shredded jicama or kohlrabi
5 tbsp. (3¾ Br. tbsp.) vinaigrette
1 tsp. (¾ Br. tsp.) chopped capers

*Arrange spears of Belgian endive and slices of
prosciutto alternately, pinwheel-style, around a
platter. (A white or clear platter is most striking.)
Pile the shredded radicchio and jicama, or kohlrabi,
in the center.*

*In a small mixing bowl, whisk the vinaigrette with
the capers and drizzle it over the whole arrangement.
Serve with plates and forks.*

37

Cream of Sunchoke Soup

1 tbsp. (¾ Br. tbsp.) lemon juice
1 lb. Jerusalem artichokes (sunchokes)
1 tbsp. (¾ Br. tbsp.) butter
3 cloves garlic, minced
2½ cups (20 fl. oz.) vegetable stock
½ cup (4 fl. oz.) milk
2 bay leaves
½ cup (4 fl. oz.) light cream
salt and pepper

Add lemon juice to a bowl of cold water. Peel and dice sunchokes. Place in lemon-water to prevent discoloration. Meanwhile, melt butter in a stockpot over medium heat. Add garlic and cook, stirring, for 3 minutes. Drain sunchokes, add to stockpot, stirring and cooking another 3 minutes. Stir in stock, milk and bay leaves. Cover and simmer 20 to 30 minutes until sunchokes are fork-tender. Remove bay leaves. Purée soup, then put through a sieve. Return to heat, stir in cream, and add salt and pepper to taste. Serves 2 to 4.

"These things are not substitutes for tame foods. They have flavors of their own, and it is not fair to them to call them by the name of something else."

Euell Gibbons, on Jerusalem artichokes

Bok Choy Stir-Fry

4-6 stalks bok choy (inside stalks)
1 tbsp. (¾ Br. tbsp.) vegetable oil
3 cloves garlic, minced
½ red bell pepper, sliced
¼ cup (2 fl. oz.) sherry
2 tbsp. (1½ Br. tbsp.) soy sauce
1 tbsp. (¾ Br. tbsp.) Thai garlic chili pepper sauce,
    or to taste
1½ cups (12 fl. oz.) savory cabbage, shredded
1½ cups (12 fl. oz.) mushrooms, sliced (try oyster,
    enoki, button)
¼ cup (2 fl. oz.) peanuts
salt and pepper to taste

*Separate ribs from leaves of bok choy. Dice ribs
and coarsely chop the leaves. Have all other vegetables ready. You should have about 5 to 6 cups
(40-48 fl. oz.) raw vegetables. Heat wok or skillet
over high heat. Add oil and garlic, then bok choy
ribs and red bell pepper. Cook 1 minute, stirring
constantly. Add sherry and soy sauce. Cover and
cook 2 minutes more. Remove cover and stir in
garlic chili pepper sauce. Add bok choy leaves,
cabbage and mushrooms. Cook 1 to 2 minutes,
stirring, until leaves wilt. Add peanuts and salt
and pepper. Serves 4.*

Grilled Exotic Vegetables

1 head radicchio
1 head Belgian endive
1 red bell pepper
1 Japanese eggplant
6 oyster or shiitake mushrooms
1 fennel bulb, blanched
¼ tsp. crushed red pepper
1 tbsp. (¾ Br. tbsp.) balsamic vinegar
2 tbsp. (1½ Br. tbsp.) olive oil
1 tsp. (¾ Br. tsp.) sugar
1 tsp. (¾ Br. tsp.) lemon juice
4 cloves garlic, crushed

Wash and trim vegetables, removing any cores, seeds and stems. Cut the Belgian endive lengthwise in half. Cut the eggplant diagonally into ½-inch slices and salt both sides. Let slices sit on paper towels for 15 minutes, then blot dry. Cut the radicchio and blanched fennel into quarters and spear the layers with a toothpick so they will hold together when grilling. Cut the red pepper into 2-inch wedges. When all the vegetables have been prepared, spread them out in a single layer on a platter.

In a mixing bowl, whisk together the remaining ingredients and brush mixture over both sides of the vegetables. Let them marinate for at least 10 minutes.

Meanwhile, prepare the grill. When grill is hot, coat it with vegetable spray to prevent sticking. Grill veg-

*etables a few minutes on each side (the fennel needs
the longest time; the mushrooms need the least time),
basting them with olive oil when necessary. Serves 4.*

Exotic Mushroom Omelet

1 cup (8 fl. oz.) sliced raw exotic mushrooms
3 tbsp. (2¼ Br. tbsp.) butter
1 clove garlic, peeled and halved
2 sprigs fresh savory
4 eggs
2 tbsp. (1½ Br. tbsp.) water
salt and pepper
2-3 oz. Camembert cheese, rind removed, cut into pieces

*In a skillet over medium heat, melt 1 tbsp.
(¾ Br. tbsp.) butter. Add the garlic and savory, then
the mushrooms; cook, stirring constantly until the
mushrooms are tender. Spoon mushrooms into a
small bowl lined with paper towel to absorb excess
moisture; remove garlic and savory.*

*Return skillet to medium heat and melt 2 tbsp.
(1½ Br. tbsp.) butter. Meanwhile, beat the eggs with
the water. Add salt and pepper as desired. Pour eggs
into prepared skillet. When the eggs are almost set,
add the cheese to half the omelet, then add the mushrooms on top of the cheese. Cook until the cheese just
starts to melt, about 1 minute. Fold the omelet and
slide onto a plate. Serves 2.*

Shrimp Salad with Papaya

2 cups (16 fl. oz.) shrimp, cooked and peeled
¾ cup (6 fl. oz.) celery, diced
½ cup (4 fl. oz.) shredded coconut
2 papayas, cut lengthwise in slices, seeds removed
½ cup (4 fl. oz.) mayonnaise
½ cup (4 fl. oz.) sour cream
1 tsp. (¾ Br. tsp.) curry powder
1 tsp. (¾ Br. tsp.) lime juice
1 tsp. (¾ Br. tsp.) sugar
2 tbsp. (1½ Br. tbsp.) mango or other chutney
salt and pepper to taste

In a medium-sized bowl mix all ingredients together except the papaya. Spoon mixture over the papaya slices. Serve with a slice of lime. Serves 4.

Mango Chutney

1 cup (8 fl. oz.) brown sugar
½ cup (4 fl. oz.) cider vinegar
1½ cups (12 fl. oz.) mango, peeled and chopped
1 tbsp. (¾ Br. tbsp.) candied preserved ginger, chopped
3 oz. raisins
1 cinnamon stick
12 whole cloves
½ tsp. whole coriander seeds

In a medium saucepan bring the vinegar and sugar to a boil. Add the remaining ingredients, with the spices tied up in a cheesecloth bag. Simmer uncovered, stirring occasionally, about 1 hour. When mixture has thickened, remove spice bag. Cool, cover and refrigerate. Makes 1½ cups (12 fl. oz.).

"*Here are fruits, flowers,
leaves, and branches,
And here is my heart
which beats only for you.*"
PAUL VERLAINE
Romances sans paroles

Kiwi Meringues

2 egg whites
¼ tsp. salt
½ tsp. cream of tartar
½ tsp. vanilla extract
½ cup (4 fl. oz.) sugar
6 kiwis, peeled and sliced
vanilla ice cream or frozen yogurt
papaya sauce, opt.

Preheat oven to 250°F. Cover a cookie sheet with brown paper. In a mixing bowl, beat the egg whites until they are frothy and begin to hold their shape. Add the salt, cream of tartar and vanilla, and beat slightly. Then add the sugar very gradually (about 1 tbsp. at a time), beating well after each addition until stiff peaks form. With a rubber spatula, drop the meringue mixture onto the paper-lined cookie sheet, forming 6 separate nest shapes with the edges slightly raised. Bake meringues about 1 hour until dry. Carefully remove them from the paper with a spatula and turn them upside down. Return them to the oven 5 more minutes to complete drying. Let them cool on a rack.

Serve each meringue with a scoop of ice cream or frozen yogurt topped by the slices from one kiwi. For a softly colorful effect, drizzle papaya sauce over kiwis.

Papaya Sauce

1 tsp. (¾ Br. tsp.) cornstarch
¼ cup (2 fl. oz.) sugar
¼ cup (2 fl. oz.) water
1 tsp. (¾ Br. tsp.) lemon juice
¼ tsp. vanilla extract
¾ cup (6 fl. oz.) crushed papayas
1 tsp. (¾ Br. tsp.) brandy (opt.)

In a small saucepan, bring all ingredients to a boil, stirring frequently until mixture thickens. Let cool, then purée sauce in a blender or food processor. Cover and chill. Drizzle over fresh fruit, ice cream or sorbet.

Guava Sorbet

2 cups (16 oz.) guava or feijoa pulp
2 tbsp. (1½ Br. tbsp.) lemon juice
1 cup (8 fl. oz.) sugar
1 cup (8 fl. oz.) water

In a saucepan combine sugar and water. Bring to a boil and cook 5 minutes. Purée pulp, removing seeds if desired. Add lemon juice. Mix with sugar syrup. Pour into a pan and cover with foil. Freeze until firm. Break into pieces and process until just slushy. Place in a covered container and freeze again until firm. Serve at room temperature, when slightly softened. Serves 4 to 6.

Passionate Smoothie

2 ripe passion fruits
1 ripe banana or pepino, peeled and seeded
1 cup (8 fl. oz.) frozen vanilla yogurt or ice cream
½ cup (4 fl. oz.) milk

Place passion fruit pulp and pepino or banana in a blender or food processor, and process until smooth. Strain out passion fruit seeds. Add frozen yogurt and milk, and blend. Makes two 6-oz. servings.

46

*"And the fruits will outdo
what the flowers have promised!"*

François de Malherbe

Graphic Design by Gretchen Goldie

Photo Styling by Sue Tallon

Acknowledgments

Max Bromwell, Paul Costa, Evalyn Dail,
Susan Dinsmore, Ruth Hanks, Jean Hyde,
Lisa Kraisriwatana, Lisa Palmire,
Joe Poshek, Bill and Robin Smith,
Juliette Trygg, and Julie Tumpney

some produce courtesy of
Frieda's Rare and Exotic Foods, Los Angeles, CA.